# Spiritual
# Discernment

# Spiritual Discernment

## Watchman Nee

CHRISTIAN FELLOWSHIP PUBLISHERS, INC.
NEW YORK

ISBN: 978-0-935008-91-3

*Available from the Publishers at:*

11515 Allecingie Parkway
Richmond, Virginia 23235
www.c-f-p.com

Printed in the United States of America

# FOREWORD

Listen to the prayer of the apostle Paul for his beloved church in Philippi: "this I pray, that your love may abound yet more and more in knowledge and all discernment; so that ye may approve the things that are excellent; that ye may be sincere and void of offence unto the day of Christ" (Philippians 1:9-10). What was it that inspired him to offer such a prayer for the dear saints in Philippi? Do we today desperately need the same prayer? We talk about love and fellowship, and yet we encounter many problems and failures. What is the missing link to a glorious church? Can it be the lack of "full knowledge and all perception that ye may prove [or, distinguish] the things that differ" (literal translation)?

Certainly spiritual discernment is the pressing need of today. How can we obtain this full knowledge of God? Where do we get spiritual discernment that we may know the things which differ or are more excellent? These are the matters which brother Watchman Nee tried to address during his latter years of ministry.

This present volume, entitled *Spiritual Discernment* is composed of three parts: Abound in Knowledge, Abound in Discernment, and Approve the Excellent. The Publishers were able to acquire these Notes in Chinese recently, and they have now been translated into English for sharing with the English-speaking saints.

May these Notes help many in meeting the pressing need of today.

# SPIRITUAL DISCERNMENT

# PART ONE: ABOUND IN KNOWLEDGE

*"This I pray, that your love may abound yet more and more in knowledge ..."*

Philippians 1.9

## Chapter 1

## THE SPIRIT-CONTROLLED SOUL

The mind is the most active part of the soul. It used to be like a wild horse, but now it is being restrained by the will. And the will is in cooperation with the spirit.

The way to a spirit-controlled soul comes about as follows: At the moment when the mind begins to think of questionable things and to wander, the first step of control is to discern, that is, to see the condition of the mind in the light of God. The second step is to drive out or cast aside such unhealthy thoughts. And the third step is to return to quietness in God's presence. Then, begin to prove — under the light received what are the permissible, even the acceptable, thoughts of God.

Emotion is the lowest, the most unreasonable, part of the soul; yet it exerts the greatest power in swaying the will. Whatever emotion is attached to, the will will usually agree. For emotion acts like a favored child who always gets what he wants with a few cries before his mother. It almost seems that the entire life of a person is controlled by emotion: by what it likes or seeks after. Indeed, its like or dislike is rather irrational. However, if it comes under the control of the spirit, it cannot act so independently as it wishes. It has to yield to God's approval or permission, though it will always strive against God's wish. This is the striving between the spirit and the flesh. It causes the greatest pain to the soul. For the soul is not able to like what emotion naturally likes of a person, thing or affair. There in the very depth of man is something that desires after God. But emotion longs after things, and the mind frequently rationalizes and supports emotion. Thus, man is unable to live peacefully. If he is able to disregard his emotion and lay down his like, he will have peace. This does not mean that God will not permit us to like any person, thing or affair. What He seeks to do is to get rid of the natural source of such like or dislike — that is, to eliminate such independent choice. It will be right if there be no independent preference but rather there be delight in what God loves, in what person, thing or affair God takes pleasure in. Such is the spirit-controlled emotion. For the spirit lays hold of man's emotion by exercising his will. Emotion is an irrational force; yet so also is the Holy Spirit a powerful force above reason. When emotion fails to be satisfied, it causes man to feel uncomfortable and unhappy. So also will the Holy Spirit be grieved when His demand is neglected, thus causing man the loss of peace and joy. Unless a person obeys the spirit and lets his emotion suffer, he will not regain peace and joy.

Will is the highest faculty of the soul, yet it occupies only a small portion of the soul. For our life is habitually controlled by emotion and mind. The will seems to permit whatever emotion delights in. And when the mind seems to so logically argue, the will will likewise go along. As soon as the will decides, action immediately follows suit. Hence, sinning is an act of the will. What God and Satan contend over is the will of man. Accordingly, the will is the center or crux of man. What the will inclines towards is what man moves forward about. We cannot be complacent about this.

A spirit-controlled will inclines towards God's will. It unites with God's will, seeks after Him, and is able to rise above one's own emotion and reasoning. A submissive will pleases God immensely, for He can use it to hold sway over the whole man.[*]

---

[*] Notes from a message given on March 28, 1949.

## Chapter 2

## RISEN FROM AMONG THE DEAD

- A Christian, living in the spirit, is already a factual matter, even though his body yet waits to be resurrected.

- Resurrection commences Christian life.

- All that should die in Adam has died, is buried in the tomb, never to rise again.

- What is risen is only what belongs to resurrection, for the old has once and for all passed away.

- All Christian man's thoughts and intents are new (see Rom. 6.4).

- His relationship with God as well as his relationship with people, things and affairs are all new.

- He can experientially resist all the things of the flesh because he has died in Adam. He can therefore draw upon "the dying power of Jesus" (see 2 Cor. 4.10) to deal with and put to death the flesh when the latter is discovered in the light. The man in Christ is dead to sin, so he sins no more. The "dying of Jesus" becomes a power in his life.

- Like a beloved child of God, the Christian lives only to God. He does His will and pleases Him in all things. He walks before God according to the measure of light he has. He is a heavenly man living among men. Death can no longer touch him, and Satan has no place in him.

- Christian man's problem lies in the fact that resurrection is not strong enough in him; therefore, he has not been able to live in the power of this resurrection life, and his death to sin is not thorough. May I shout to all Christians: "Do you know that you are risen from the dead? that Christ is now your life?" For in Christ, old things are passed away; behold, all things are become new (see 2 Cor. 5.17).

- May this resurrection be registered in our mind, even in our subconsciousness, so that we may always sense and believe that we have been risen from among the dead. May our speech, attitude and action in all things reveal that we are resurrected people.*

---

* Notes from a message given on March 31, 1949.

## Chapter 3

## THE ASCENT OF THE SOUL

The standard for today's living for the Christian is the life of God within. It is the nature of the Lord's life. This is the source of living. It has within it the law of ascending — that is to say, the law of the ascending of the soul. Its actions can be likened to an experiment in physics involving the ascending of water in a series of water pipes. When water is first poured into the pipes, you notice that the water level in the pipe remotest from the source is at the lowest. But gradually the water level there begins to rise till it becomes level with the source.

In like manner, when the condition of the soul is not level with the resurrection life of Christ, the law of life has the power to uplift the soul till it becomes level to that life or is able to manifest that life. Therefore, when the inward and the outward are different, the law of ascent will begin to operate, causing you to feel spiritually undone, uncomfortable and restless. Not until the inward and the outward become one will you gain spiritual peace and harmony.

(1) When the spirit and the soul are intertwined, the soul always dominates and the spirit is under its influence. Whenever something happens, the entire man will launch forth and express itself. Here, the spirit is unclean, for it is contaminated by the soul. And hence, frequently, bad temper, impatience and other evils will burst forth.

(2) But with the *dividing* of the soul and the spirit, the soul can be busily engaged, even reproving others with strong words, yet the spirit remains quiet and unperturbed.

Given this scenario, the action of the soul takes on the appearance of a theatrical play, for there is a distance between the spirit and the soul. Yet, such "dramatic scenes" are dependent upon whether or not the soul is under the control of the spirit; for one cannot say that when the soul is sinning, the spirit is able to maintain its composure without being affected.

(3) The spirit and the soul take action together in a straight line.*

---

* Notes from a message given on March 2, 1949.

## Chapter 4

## CHRIST IS THE WAY

"Jesus saith unto him, I am the way, and the truth, and the life: no man cometh unto the Father, but by me" (John 14.6).

"Enter ye in by the narrow gate: for wide is the gate, and broad is the way, that leadeth to destruction, and many are they that enter in thereby. For narrow is the gate, and straitened the way, that leadeth unto life, and few are they that find it" (Matt. 7.13-14).

- Christ is the way in searching the Scriptures.

- Christ is the way for one's life—in every stage of his life.

- Christ is the way of living: living daily according to the Lord's nature within.

- Christ is the way in ministry; the latter is not based on worldly education, ethics, teaching and law. Ministry is telling people what you really know. Only what has been wrought within a person can be considered as God's work. What has touched the Lord or what comes from His touch may alone be reckoned to be the things of God. And as you speak, the Holy Spirit begins to work in men's heart. All who have eyes to see will see it.[*]

---

[*] Notes from a message given on April 3, 1949.

## Chapter 5

## THE NEW CREATION

- The new creation spoken of in II Corinthians 5:17 constitutes the union of God himself with His creation.

- The first new creation is Jesus Christ (Immanuel; i.e. "God with us" see Matthew 1:23b). Jesus is sinless; therefore, He can use His flesh to bear the sin of the world.

- This truly is the new creation (a being comprised of the union of God and man), which the world had never seen before.

- The second new creation—a circle of people—is the Church, the Body of Christ. These people were sinful, but their sin problem is solved by the death of the first new creation.

- The Church as the new creation commences at the resurrection, although God's beginning of the new creation in this universe commenced at Bethlehem.

- The first new creation is purely holy, untainted by sin. The second new creation was formerly dead in sin, and therefore it needed the first new creation to go to the cross, shed blood to solve the sin problem before it became the new creation: before it could be united with God. Thus, the only-begotten Son has become the firstborn of many sons.

- The differences between the new creation and the old original creation are as follows:

- All things in the old creation are separated from the Creator, whereas everything in the new creation is joined to the Creator.

- Things of the old creation are perishable and decaying, but things belonging to the new creation can neither die nor be corrupted.

- Only what is in the new creation can manifest God's glory eternally. This characteristic is lacking in the old creation.

- At the moment the Lord died, all within the original creation received its judgment. (Original creation is represented by the Cherubim which appeared on the veil of the Temple — see Mark 15:38, Luke 23:45).

- At the time of the future restoration, the old creation shall be revived.[*]

---

[*] Notes from a message given on April 6, 1949.

Chapter 6

# THE GODLY HAVE A TENDER SPIRIT

- Whenever the godly encounter words from God, from the Bible, from the Holy Spirit or from reality, they will bow their heads and gladly receive such words, even if they should come out of the mouth of a child.

- The godly will give words heard careful consideration, even thinking according to the speaker's thought; yet they will never compromise.

- But in the end, the godly will pay more attention to the speaker's spirit than to his thoughts and reasoning; for they realize that logic may sound right but the speaker's spirit can be wrong.[*]

---

[*] Notes from a message given on April 11, 1949.

## Chapter 7

## WHAT IS GOD'S WORD?

What is the word of God? People usually consider commands or the law to be God's word. They accept Proverbs, words of experience, and ordinances in the Bible as the word of God. The Bible is His word. According to our thinking, God's word should not have any human element in it. Nevertheless, men's experiences and human histories are in His word — the Bible. For the latter includes not just commands. What man has been touched by God is also written in the Bible. Paul in 2 Corinthians 2.4 said the following: "out of much affliction and anguish of heart I wrote unto you with many tears; not that ye should be made sorry, but that ye might know the love which I have more abundantly unto you." This is human feeling, yet it is also God's word. Hence, the Bible contains human element. In the Old Testament we see that God's word includes within it the human element. And when it came to Christ in the New Testament, God's word became flesh. This was absolutely impossible with respect to the Old Testament saints; for not all human elements in the men of the Old Testament were usable. Such would either leak away or contaminate God's word. Man is therefore God's restriction and hindrance. Yet in Christ Jesus all His human elements were for God. This is the only man who neither restricts nor hinders God's word. For the first time we have the standard for the ministry of God's word, which is (a) that God is willing to speak and (b) that unless there is human element, we will never be able to comprehend what God is saying.

Let us take, for example, the matter of holiness: it appears differently in any two persons. But when the Lord says, "Be you holy," we begin to understand what holiness is because here in Jesus himself is the standard of holiness. The standard is Christ, and the way to reach that standard is also Christ. God's word is in Him, and the substance of the word of God is also in Him. What God's word says is found in Him. The Lord says, "I am meek and lowly in heart". This substance called meekness is in Him. Indeed, He is that very substance. To whatever degree the word of God says, to that very degree is the substance of it in Him. None of God's word is merely objective. All is subjective. Where His word is, there is the substance. God makes the abstract substantial. You do not just hear the word, you see it as well.

What is the ministry of God's word? When the word is written, the substance behind the word follows suit. Though the word has passed through man's being, it nonetheless remains pure. It is still the living water. Each time God's word is given, there is the living water, subjective and substantial. For this reason, what dealings must we go through! When a brother talks about holiness, does he give you a sense of holiness? Or when he speaks on the Holy Spirit, will it impress you with a sense of the flesh? What God looks for is not how correct your message is, but how correct your life is.[*]

---

[*] Notes on a message given on May 31, 1949.

## Chapter 8

## How to Diagnose (or Discern)

Upon your having an impression in the spirit, it needs your mind to interpret or understand it; otherwise, you have no way to help others. God's spirit of judgment or discernment in our spirit has a double use: (a) our spirit becomes usable, and (b) we are able to recognize another's spirit. For our ability to know the spirit in another person does not come from books, nor from the experiences of older saints, but from our personal dealings before God. It may be that you sense something moving in another's spirit and feel uneasy about it; yet you fail to know why it is so. This is because the spiritual judgment you may have acquired thus far is inadequate. But if you have been dealt with by God in such condition sufficiently, you will then be able to pinpoint the cause. Touching another's spirit and the ability to tell why are two different things. You need both to point out the sin committed and assess the cause of the trouble. If God has thoroughly judged me and disciplined me, then I have learned before Him that such and such a spirit is an expression of self-love, pride or jealousy. And so, as soon as a person shows self-love or pride, I know the case and am able to judge. We need a workable spirit by which to diagnose another's spirit. Our learning should therefore be broad, in that we ourselves need to be widely judged. The more dealings we receive before God, the more discernments we will have. Oftentimes, we can indeed recognize people's faults, yet we cannot help because our own dealings are not thorough enough.

If you have learned deeply with respect to the lesson of pride, you will instantly detect the rise in yourself of any tiny self-satisfaction or self-glory: you know at once that you want people to pay attention to you: your pride draws people's notice and you are well satisfied with yourself. Spiritual insight is different from simply picking out faults in yourself. You must not just sense it, you must also be able to explain it. How much sin the church allows to remain depends on what measure of sin you permit in your own life. Should the most hidden sins in you be judged, you have learned deeply.

In the case of weeping, is it because of self-love, because of pain, or because of being broken by God? Weeping is a sign of weakness, we weep because we are beaten. Some people do not know how to weep. This is due to their lack of feeling. The most difficult group of Christians is that of those who have never been poured from vessel to vessel. They have never submitted, have never bowed down, have never been softened. Everything which happens has to gratify their hearts. They cannot endure the tiniest frustration. You therefore know that such people have received little grace, and hence you cannot commit any church affairs to them. The cross has not worked in their lives. Bad temper in them is due to either pride or self-love. Nevertheless, if you yourself have received dealings in such areas, you will be able to deal with them with spiritual discernment.

A person with much discipline but little learning is a hard person. He is unable to yield. He has dealings but no lessons learned, much discipline yet no good results. But if much discipline is coupled with a tender spirit, you should expect to see much result. Yet strangely, the spirit is still poor. The probable reason is that people despise things spiritual. Furthermore, if the spirit is tender and there is not the belittlement of spiritual things and yet there is still the lack of fruit, then this you realize is the lack of the supply of God's word.

So, to be useful in discernment requires that (a) you know how to use your spirit and (b) you know how to help others.

We need to recognize the source from where things come; otherwise, we shall be deceived.[*]

---

[*] Note: Date unknown.

*Chapter 9*

## A MINISTER OF THE WORD

What is preaching? We shall see that there are three different approaches.

> "Now on the last day, the great day of the feast, Jesus stood and cried, saying, If any man thirst, let him come unto me and drink. He that believeth on me, as the scripture hath said, from within him [Gr. *out of his belly*] shall flow rivers of living water" (John 7.37-38 margin).

God speaks through the mouth of man. Should God's word be eliminated from the world, there will not be much work left to be done. We should know the place of God's word in His work. His work is full of His word. And these words are uttered by human mouths. Here we have the ministers of the word of God. Without word, there will not be God's work. Without ministers, there also will not be any work. God can speak in various ways. We assume that when God speaks, He himself speaks. But if one looks in the Bible, it would appear that God often refuses to speak directly; rather, He will speak through His ministers.

(1) Regarding the Old Testament ministers, they needed to have vision. Even the prophecies of Balaam are considered to be major ones. It seems that God put a stop to Balaam's thoughts, feelings and opinions. Then he was enabled to pass on the word of God with purity and accuracy. In the matter of revelations during the Old Testament period, it would appear that the place of man was

kept at the lowest level. Moses worked for the most part on the same principle as that of Balaam, in that he did not add any of his words to God's word. Nevertheless, there was a difference. Anything which proceeded from Balaam himself was condemned (this is evident from the story of Balaam throughout God's book of revelation), but some of the words which Moses uttered revealed his own feeling as well as that of God. God could acknowledge that what Moses said was correct. So, too, was it in the case of Isaiah, David and Jeremiah. The nearer to the time of the New Testament, the more God acknowledged the words spoken by the prophets themselves.

(2) Our Lord Jesus is the word of God clothed with flesh. Whatever He does or says is the ministry of God's word. His preaching of God's word differs from Old Testament preaching. The Old Testament pronouncement was God speaking through the voice of man. But the Lord Jesus is the word of God become flesh, thus including both man and word. During the Old Testament period word was word and man was man, with God merely using the mouth of man. We see in the New Testament period, however, that it is God's word clothed with human flesh. The word becomes the man. Such a minister of God's word is totally different. For here the word has human feeling, thought and opinion, and yet it is still God's word. In Old Testament times any intrusion of man's thought and feeling would have defiled the word of God and made it impure. In order to maintain its purity, no human thought and feeling could enter into it. However, in the life of the Lord Jesus, it is altogether different. For in God's word there now came the entrance into it of human thought, feeling and opinion, and yet it did not fail to be God's word. The thought of the Lord is the thought of God. The feeling of the Lord is the feeling

of God. God does not want to have His word only, He also wants His word to have personality — with thought, feeling and opinion added into it. Here we find that God's word is no longer totally objective but is also subjective, for it contains human feeling, thought and opinion. Nonetheless, it is still the word of God. Accordingly, we discover here a great principle: that man's feeling does not adversely affect God's word, nor will man's thought hinder it.

The issue hinges on man's thought. What kind of thought is it? In the Lord's life, God's word is perfected by the Lord's thought. It is so much nobler than the Old Testament experience: "Ye have heard that it was said to them of old times," declared Jesus, "but I say unto you ..." (Matthew 5:21a, 22a). You see here that the Old Testament is not destroyed; rather, it is raised higher by the Lord to perfection. The word of God has not only sound but also thought and feeling in our Lord. The word has become a Person.

Formerly God's word had no personality, today it has personality in the life of the Lord Jesus. Man's word becomes God's word. Man's word and God's word join into one. Here is a minister of the word who is altogether subjective. When the Old Testament prophets spoke, theirs were the words of God. But even when the Lord Jesus is *silent*, there still is the word of God. This is an advance from revelation to personality. In the Old Testament period word was word and man was man. But in the New Testament period word becomes flesh. This man's word is God's word. He has no need for revelation, since whatever this man feels or thinks is the feeling and thought of God. In the life of the Lord Jesus, God's word is not in the least jeopardized by man; it is instead perfectly expressed by him. He truly is the minister of the word of God.

(3) The ministry to be found in the New Testament record has the character of Christ as well as that of the Old Testament revelation. In the life of the Lord Jesus there is first God's word and then comes the flesh to fit in together with the word. But now there is the flesh first, and then in order to be a minister of God's word the latter will transform the flesh in order to fit it in with God's word. And thus, the minister of the New Testament word is one having God's revelation plus the elements of man's thought, feeling and opinion added in. God will deal with man's thought, feeling, cleverness and all other human features in order to release His word. So that a New Testament minister is one whose flesh is being so dealt with that the word of God might be manifested.

God can speak in four different ways: (a) He can speak directly by himself so that there is absolute purity without any error. (b) God can use nature through which to speak— such as by thunder, loud and clear. (c) He can speak through angels; although He does not use angels to preach and deliver articles of faith but uses them only as messengers. And (d) God can use a gramophone by which to speak, speaking mechanically without any error.

Yet, instead of using these ways He prefers to speak through the mouth of man. In so doing, however, He faces the greatest danger; for man is independent and sinful, having his own thoughts and intents. Allowing man to be His mouthpiece, God takes the greatest risk. Yet He purposes to have His word conveyed with human elements. Instead of using those more dependable risk-free ways, He delights in having man to speak for Him. He intends to turn the human element into supporting the word of God instead of hindering it. Though He faces great danger in choosing man, this will make His word higher and fuller because human feeling, thought and opinion may be added to the word without changing its purity or accuracy. So, today God's word is manifested in human terms. Each person God uses has his own style, with his special vocabulary. For example, what vocabulary Luke used was different from that of Matthew. John had his signs and was so different in vocabulary from the words used by Paul. This indicates how the word of God is greatly manifested with the addition of human elements. Such is the standard of ministry.

God looks for subjectivity. In the Gospel of Mark, it is replete with the use of "immediately" as one of its key words. Matthew pays special attention to "the grace of the Lord"; and so he uses great numbers. His personal thoughts and language characteristics are being used by God. Indeed, God's use of man's characteristics is a hallmark of the New Testament minister. God does not want to eliminate human thought and feeling so as to make of him a machine or robot. He would rather work in man to such an extent as to be able to make use of the human element. For such will add to the completeness, power and beauty of God's word. Because God will use your usable thoughts but reject your unusable ones, what dealings you must go through! God also desires to use our feelings, but some are serviceable and some are not. So He will discipline us. For if there be no discipline, there will be no minister. God wants His word to be clothed in flesh. He wants His word to touch and discipline man before it is released to others. Oh, how unlike Balaam or even unlike the principle of tongues: Paul forbade speaking in tongues in the church if there be no interpretation.

The "belly" is that part of man at the depth of his entire being. God uses man's innermost being, not merely a canal nor channel. We need to drink deeply of the Lord, and out of our innermost depths shall flow rivers of living waters (see again John 7.38). It needs to be asked: How much living water poured through one's "belly" is still living? Unfortunately, many living waters become dead waters after they have passed through a man's innermost depths. A minister of God's word is to be the channel for giving living waters to people. The ministry of the word is not merely objective, for the word is the living water that has come forth after having first been thoroughly digested within the minister himself. God does not want mere objective ministry: His word must have the human element (the "belly" element) in it but without the danger of there being any loss. With the New Testament apostles each had his personal characteristics added in, and yet the word of God was able to come forth gloriously. God's word proceeds not only from the mouth of man, but has first passed through the man's feeling, thought and opinion in such a way that its glory has remained intact. If, however, there be uncleanness and hindrance, the word of God will naturally suffer loss.[*]

---

[*] Message given on May 30, 1934.

## Chapter 10

## A USABLE SPIRIT

My spirit, when attempting to help another believer, is impure whenever my undealt-with self is involved in the spirit's release. I am not objective enough. It will be like a physician who becomes angry at the sickness of the sick one. As long as my undisciplined feeling enters in, my spirit turns impure. There are two ways which leave the spirit impure: (a) my undisciplined self is let loose, and (b) though I have indeed been disciplined, this time when I speak I allow my self-life to become involved. To correct the first of these two ways, I need the basic dealing of God. It cannot be remedied by any other measure. And with respect to the second way—in which, even though I have experienced brokenness I am nonetheless unwittingly affected by the self of my brother resulting in my spirit coming forth contaminated—I must stop immediately and confess that I am wrong: I must restrain my spirit, laying it aside without trying to repair it. Indeed, I should condemn it and not attempt to redeem it. I should judge it and return to normal.

Some people's thoughts are not pliable. They are difficult to be turned to God. As soon as they have their thought, they are bound by them. Such people are most subjective. They need time to be readjusted. They need the help of the church. For what the church does is in accordance with the decision of God. The strength of any one person is limited. Your body is your limit as well as your standard. But God is omnipotent, and He delegates His authority to the church, the body of Christ. Yet, today, what God is able to do is limited by the measure of the church.

God certainly obtained a body through His Son; nonetheless, the church has become God's limitation as well as His measure.

Subjectivity makes a person the measure, and thus he is unable to accept the measure of the church. It is therefore essential for brethren to learn to accept the judgment of the church. This will deliver us from subjectivity.

On the one hand, unpliable thought cannot be moved by either the church or the Spirit of God. On the other hand, the more you submit yourself to authority the less you will find fault with the church and the more you shall be blessed. But the more you find fault and the spiritually drier you shall become.

Learn to accept the discipline of the Holy Spirit, and then your spirit will be purified. You have no need to know how correct your spirit is; you simply need to know when your spirit is wrong. We must have a spirit marked by trembling and fear lest we be wrong. When we are really wrong, the Lord will condemn us within and the church will judge us without.

Whatever is of the spirit will possess the following characteristics: (a) the spirit's sense may be slow but grows in strength, (b) it comes from the depth within, (c) it gives us inward peace, and (d) it soothes our feeling.

Whatever comes from the undealt self bears these traits: (a) it is tempestuous and exerts pressure, (b) it allows the outward man to enter in, (c) the inward man lacks peace, and (d) it is full of reasons and self-righteousness.[*]

Through discipline, the outcome will be:
For the spirit:
Peace in the depth
For the self:
It is subdued

[*] Notes from a message given on May 28, 1949.

## Chapter 11

# THE TRAINING OF THE SPIRIT

When I try to discern the condition of another's spirit, how do I know that his spirit is wrong and mine is right? How do I conclude that his spirit has not been released? Is my own spirit up to standard? If my spirit is below standard, then I cannot make the right judgment. It is very wrong for many who judge people while they themselves have not been judged. People usually judge according to knowledge, but we must judge by the spirit. We need first of all to have no confidence in our spirit. Like a balance with different measures, our spirit itself must first be adjusted or corrected. Therefore, let us not place confidence in ourselves too early. The only reason we may judge is because we have first been judged by God. The way God trains us for future service is to let us learn first through dealings. The sensitivity of my spirit is based on my experience of when I am dealt with by God. If my spirit is released and God says it was wrong and I learn from that experience, only then can I say wrong to my brethren when their spirits come forth in like manner. No one can judge out of knowledge. Objective judgment is useless here, only subjective discernment acquired through discipline is useful. I can judge only according to what I myself have been judged by God. My judgment can never surpass God's judgment of me. Otherwise, it will be objective in nature. The more we receive the discipline of the Holy Spirit and are broken, the better we can discern. The legitimacy of my judgment depends on the discipline I have received. Because I have been disciplined, I use the light acquired thereby to judge others. This is God's judgment. There is no self hidden behind nor personal feeling involved. In case there is something in me that has not been judged, I cannot judge or discern when this very thing appears in others — with the result that I allow that sin to remain in my brother as well as in me.

Some may learn yet such learning may not be thorough enough. Judgment or discernment comes not from knowledge, cleverness or mind. It comes from what I have gone through myself. Since God has broken something in my life, I am able to judge. Therefore, let us not try to escape from discipline and personal dealing lest we cannot deal with other people. We need to learn deeply so that we may be useful. Whatever lesson you have learned from discipline or revelation, that very thing you will store in your spirit. He who is broken most is the richest for ministering to others. What is meant by ministry, your ministry? It means that you use what you have learned and stored in your spirit to help others. This is ministry. Let there be prayers asking the Lord to increase His judgment in me that I might be enriched, that I may appreciate what is beautiful and recognize what is problematic. The Lord will deal with my spirit daily till it becomes dependable.

Several possible conditions may appear in man. If you are able to touch only one of them, your help will not be thorough enough. You must allow God to do His work freely in you. A medical doctor may become a physician without himself being sick, but a spiritual physician must begin with having sickness himself. Spiritual sickness one after another needs to be increased and expanded in you day by day so that there may be God's dealings with them one after another. Do not be fearful of hardships, for such will provide you many good lessons. The more frequent and stricter the discipline, the better the learning experience and the richer the spirit. There is no shortcut. A spiritual man is one who has been judged more and more. And hence, being more sensitive, he will discern things which are wrong most quickly.

The Lord is looking for dependable people. The more the discipline, the better the standard of discernment. How do I know which kind of Christian is right? People who have received more discipline are the most reliable. For there will come forth worthy diagnosis and judgment. We need to know our own selves. If we have learned to know ourselves aright, we will be capable of dealing with all men. Humans are all almost alike. You yourself qualify as a representative. There is the seed of sin in all of us. Human nature in all of us is nearly alike. It is hard to find anyone who is altogether different. The difference is merely in the growing into fruit. If you really know yourself, you will be able to deal with most any person. One's learning experience needs to be wide as well as deep so that none of what your brothers and sisters have learned will be beyond your ability to discern. God's judgment enlightens you. Each and every instance of learning will increase the light, enabling you to deal with others. But should the discipline of the Holy Spirit not be deep enough, the dealing will not be thorough and broad, thus disabling you from judging many things. And if you find yourself unable to judge, do not ever try to discern with your mind.[*]

---

[*] Notes from a message given on May 27, 1949.

# PART TWO: ABOUND IN DISCERNMENT

*"This I pray, that your love may abound yet more and more in ... all discernment ..."*

Philippians 1:9

## Chapter 1

## HOW TO DISCERN

Our Lord has a distinct quality, and that is, He knows people. He knew even Judas Iscariot that the latter was a thief. He knows everything so well that we all desire to touch merely the hem of His garment. The apostle Paul seemed to understand this special phenomenon, for he declared this: "he that is spiritual judgeth [or, *examineth*] all things, and he himself is judged [or, *examined*] of no man" (1 Cor. 2.15 margin). The standard which our Lord sets before us is very high. He wants us sinners saved by grace to have this kind of discernment such as Paul also had. Through the years, the church has been helping us in the truth. God's truth has been revealed to us progressively. But sad to say, we have made little progress. We may be able to share objective truth with others, but we are unable to share our experiences with them. Hence, the church remains poor. We need to learn a basic lesson — that is, the lesson of learning to touch spirit with our spirit.

### (1) Learn to Touch Spirit with Spirit

How do I discern or know people? If it is not by using the light of the Holy Spirit gleaned in my own experience, then my learning is yet within the mind. The Lord wants me to know people. If what is in me is bright and shining, your spirit will not be able to deceive my spirit. So touching spirit with spirit is the first lesson to learn. In the world there are many highly sensitive instruments by which to measure things. Our spirit is also a most sensitive instrument. A delicate appliance will not be affected by any other outward influence. It can be said that it is immune to outside force. God wants us to be able to discern all things. The spirit itself has tremendous power. Due to many outside influences, however, it becomes inaccurate. This is why the outward man — our self-life — needs be broken. How easy it is to mistake the outward man for the inward man. All thoughts, intents and feelings need to be dealt with before the spirit is really usable, sensitive and unaffected by outside forces. It is difficult to get through to the spirit of another. So, people may easily deceive you without your knowledge. It is extremely difficult to know people by merely listening to what they say.

The Lord has given us a spirit. It is not just for life but also for a new function. For the spirit bears not just God's nature but His sensing ability too. The spirit is for work as well as for life. It is God's will that we exercise our spirit. He has to start breaking your strongest point. If emotion is the strongest, it tends to compromise the spirit. A self-righteous person is prone to consider his opinion as the intent of the spirit. What is detrimental to the spirit is a lack in dealing with the outward man. Such lack causes the spirit to be undependable. The church today is in lack of people whose spirit is pure. A pure spirit is able to discern and give the right judgment, and it also releases power. The Lord searches for such people whose spirit is pure and deep.

After the thinking of my outward man has been broken, my spirit will respond to and approve of the right thought. Sometimes, my spirit will disapprove of a certain thought and consider it improper. The same is true with the breaking of the feeling of my outward man. I dare not follow feeling blindly. When feeling arises, the spirit within will either amen it or disapprove of it. If thought and feeling are under control, the spirit will be brightened. But if the outward man is disquieted, the spirit is unable to judge the feeling. Therefore, one must constantly learn to follow the spirit and to deal with all things which may affect it.

The spirit alone can discern. The outward man must be quieted. The spirit needs be kept fresh, living, tranquil, alert and free from outward influence. If there be any preconceived idea, it will immediately affect the judgment of the spirit. It is far easier to have a wrong spirit than engage in a wrong action. Should my spirit be impatient and irritated, its judgment will be impaired and become inaccurate. It is therefore necessary for the spirit to be tender, quiet, dependable and trustworthy. A slight self-righteousness will temper its usefulness. If my spirit is normal, it should give me a right impression. But when people's spirit comes forth, it may not be strong. It may be very weak, unable to give out much of an impression, and which also may not even be accurate. And hence, it is hard for my spirit to detect the wrong. However, if my spirit is very fresh and pure, it will still be able to have the right impression. God wants to break down the old sensitivity and bring in the new one in order to enlighten the church.[*]

## (2) A Worker Is Steadfast and Unmovable

"My beloved brethren, be ye stedfast, unmovable, always abounding in the work of the Lord, forasmuch as ye know that your labor is not vain in the Lord" (I Corinthians 15.58).

A worker is one who is stedfast and unmovable. Only one who has a firm character is serviceable. He who wavers

---

[*] Message probably given on May 25, 1949.

is useless. "Stedfast" means "set" — solid as cement. A person who frequently changes has a weak character. By nature Peter had a weak and undependable personality, whereas Paul was a steady person. Peter might utter strong words out of his emotion, though in fact he was weak and easily moved. The Father revealed the Son to Peter (see Matt. 16.17); and in this same revelation we are told that the church is to be built upon Christ revealed. Three points are mentioned: (a) foundation, (b) church, and (c) ministry. The Lord Jesus spoke first of the ministry which was to involve Peter. Petros (for Peter) in Greek means small stone or rock, whereas petra in Greek refers to a massive rock. Each and every ministry must be undertaken by a rock-like person. Five minutes earlier, Peter had received revelation from God and came to know that Jesus is the Son of God. Immediately afterwards, however, he was tempted by Satan to rebuke the Lord for His intention to go to the cross. This demonstrated the unsteadiness of Peter. Ministers must all be like pillars. Passivity is a great sin. We need to realize how great is our responsibility. To be passive indicates an unsteady character.

Paul made a firm determination while he was still in Ephesus that he would go to Jerusalem and then, he wrote, "I must also see Rome" (Acts 19.21). From chapter 19 through chapter 28 of the book of Acts, we see the road Paul took by which he accomplished his intent. He showed a spirit of steadfastness.

There are mainly three reasons why a character is weak: (a) natural affection, (b) fear of pain, and (c) human consideration. Natural affection is deceitful for it has the ability to exaggerate. Many think that Peter fell at the time of his denial of the Lord. Actually, when he declared: "Lord, with thee I am ready to go both to prison and to death" (Luke 22.33), he had already fallen. His self-confidence before the Lord is as much a fallen characteristic as was his denial later before the maid. The time when one's emotion is excited and the time when it is dejected are equally undependable. We usually consider emotional low as a sign of fallenness. In actuality, an emotional high is just as much a signal of fallenness. For human affection always leads to pretension. We say we love the brethren. But when our emotion gets low, we will not even move a finger to help. Do you measure yourself according to your emotions? Then you are a person who does not know yourself. The Lord wants you to know your heart. Only those who seek not their own pleasure are freed from fear and able to bear the cross; such a one was Job:

> "Though he slay me, yet will I trust in him" (Job 13:15a KJV). Such are the people whom Satan cannot shake.*

## (3) Know the Seriousness of Judgment
### —a Great Responsibility

In view of the fact that judgment (that is, the ability to discern) is a most difficult task and that decision-making is a great responsibility, the dealing and discipline of God is an absolute necessity. I am like a balance that needs to be tested by God innumerable times. According to my present light, I have to confess how a person such as I am can have the knowledge to make a right judgment? For no untrustworthy man is able to utter a trustworthy word. Before I can judge, I must first distrust my balance. I need to confess that being such a person as I am, I dare not make any judgment on

---

* Message given on May 25, 1949.

matters large and difficult. This is to say that I am unworthy. I must ask the Lord to deal with me. I need the Holy Spirit to discipline me time and again. According to the measure of my being judged and dealt with by God will be the measure of my judgment.

## (4) Distinguishing Things after Having an Accurate Spirit

(a) Know the difference between learning through truth and learning from discipline. Examples of learning from truth are such things as knowing the truth of baptism, the truth of the Body of Christ, and so forth. You obey the truth, pay a price, and thus you learn. Learning from discipline is different. The Holy Spirit causes you to encounter things in your daily life so that you may learn. Essential learning comes largely from what you learn through discipline. Only a small part of essential learning is derived through truth. It is therefore not enough to learn only from truth and learn nothing from discipline. Otherwise, the breaking of your outward man will be rather limited.

(b) Know the difference between learning from discipline and learning from revelation. For our spiritual education, God arranges our circumstances. It suits our need, but it usually is slow, taking possibly two to five years. Should there be any lack of light, such learning will even be slower. So, there is also the dealing through revelation. It differs from learning through truth. The dealing through truth occurs when I see the truth and begin to follow it. I do it with understanding. But when revelation comes, it is quite different. It confuses me. It strikes like lightning. And under such enlightening, I feel shameful, sorrowful and hateful of myself. Thus am I broken. Such great revelation, however, is rare. It may happen once or twice in one's life, yet it is very necessary. Such glorious revelation strikes me to the ground.

What we see gradually and changes us slowly derives from the edification of truth, but when the glorious light of revelation comes, it is quite drastic in its outcome.

(c) Know the difference between the external and the internal. Things external are those such as head covering, baptism, our need to love people, and so forth. These are the things to be done outwardly. They may not have about them the ring of spiritual reality such as is the result of the discipline of the Holy Spirit. They may instead be the result of fear without there having been any inward enlightenment associated with them. Everything about them is merely outward action. Outwardly there seems to be obedience, yet inwardly there is neither joy nor praise. It is merely enduring in obedience. On the other hand, if one is able to accept inwardly, he can glory in his weakness: he will be joyous and be able to praise. This proves that the inward, not just the outward, has been touched. What one learns can merely be outward or it can really be inward. Each time you touch people, do you touch their outside or inside? Patience is not the hallmark of Christianity, only praise is: there can be high praise in prison such as happened with Paul and Silas (see Acts 16.19-25). What the Lord looks for is not whether you have outwardly done something. You may indeed say "yes" with your lips, but only when you can say "yes" inwardly are you approved.

(d) Know the difference between discipline and reserve. Discipline is what happens to us through the circumstance arranged by the Holy Spirit. Reserve is the resulting benefit of discipline. Each discipline improves the quality of our spiritual life. Discipline can be likened to trading. It adds something to our spirit. It is a surplus. There is something added to the spirit as well as there is some improvement in its quality. If you hear of someone who has gone through much discipline, you should use your spirit to touch his spirit, seeing whether his spirit has in fact become nobler, purer, livelier and meeker. If so, then you know that his way is genuine. Sometimes, however, after a person has gone through many disciplines, you nonetheless discover that his spirit remains unclean, cold, weak and hard. This indicates that nothing has really touched him. Though he has received much discipline, nothing was thorough enough to have affected him.

(e) Discern the relationship of past life with word and with spirit. When you listen to someone's testimony, you need to discern the relationship between his word and his former life on the one hand as well as that between his spirit and his previous life on the other. For example, if he was formerly a very quick-witted person, many times his word may be changed from what it used to be before, yet his spirit has still not been delivered: he continues to look upon himself as most capable. In short, his spirit has not yet been renewed. His word has indeed condemned his past, but his spirit has not shown improvement. His word may be against his past, yet his spirit still treasures his quick-wittedness. He feels quite upbeat and believes he should be admired. His spirit yet remains on the very side he condemns. His learning the lesson is almost nil. Had there been true learning, his spirit should have demonstrated it.

(f) Distinguish between head-speaking or spirit-speaking. Learn to distinguish whether it is the head speaking or it is the spirit speaking. If our learning be in the head, we speak from the head. But if our learning is in the spirit, the word we speak may be the same yet out of our head comes forth the spirit. In that case, others will not touch your head but touch instead your spirit. We should therefore not only touch man's head but also learn to reach the thing behind the word in that person's head. What you touch tells you from where it has originated. To distinguish whether the word comes from the mind or from the spirit is an initial experience. A young man may be able to say all that an older brother has said, for to say the same word is a relatively easy thing to do; but to have the same spirit as that older brother is quite difficult: you are not able to make others touch the same thing. Great is the difference between your speaking through your head and his speaking in the spirit. If you desire to say the same word with the same spirit, you need to have the same learning. Hence, we are careful in speaking lest people fail to touch reality. There may not be much improvement in word: what is said in the tenth year may not be much different from that said in the first year, yet the spirit is different. Advance made in the spirit is true advancement. It does not matter if there be many words or few words. What really matters is whether there is improvement in the spirit. Perhaps you admire those with a bright head, but before God all is vanity.

(g) Distinguish between what is of the spirit and what is of emotion. There is a difference in distinguishing the thought and spirit from distinguishing emotion and spirit. It is comparatively easy to separate the head from the spirit but it is fairly hard to discern emotions from the spirit. Oftentimes emotion is misunderstood as spirit. For the spirit has feeling as well as knowledge. The knowledge of the spirit is quite different from the knowledge of the head. As the spirit is being touched there will be amen, but when the head is being touched the spirit cools down. Spirit amens spirit. The function of emotion differs from that of the mind. Emotion's nature resembles quite much the nature of the spirit. Man's spirit may launch out independently of the head, but it cannot be expressed without conveying emotion. The latter, however, can be released with or without the spirit.

How then, do we know whether there is spirit in the emotion or not? How can we discern? When emotion in another comes forth without spirit, the sensitive, judging spirit in me cannot find its counterpart. My spirit senses an emptiness and is not able to respond with amen. But should his spirit come forth together with his emotion, my spirit will respond with amen. Without spirit in the other person, my spirit will cool off and is thus unable to respond positively. Only when his spirit synchronizes with my spirit will there be a sense of rightness. If it is merely emotion coming forth, his own spirit will not approve and my spirit senses discomfort. So, one must attempt to discern if there is spirit behind emotion. You will feel unclean if there is no spirit within another's emotion. By that reaction you ascertain that there is no spirit. It is much harder to deal with people who live in their emotion which is void of the spirit than with those who live in their mind.

(h) Distinguish between the natural in people and what is learned before God. In their speaking, the natural condition will be exposed. There is much to learn here. For example, suppose someone naturally speaks very fast. But since he has learned some lessons before God, he will soon begin to control his word. Some have learned enough over their natural inclinations, whereas others must continue to learn how to overcome their flesh. Much disciplinary learning can turn their natural abilities into glory. Ordinarily man's nature may remain hidden during the first fifteen minutes, but it will be disclosed later on. Through cleverness, extreme heaviness or flippancy, his nature will eventually be revealed. With the exercise of restraint before God, the lesson will be learned. Let us learn in every circumstance—whether it be sickness, environment or material things. Let us learn in our attitude. Let us learn to be balanced and suitable in all things.[*]

---

[*] Message given on the evening of May 25, 1949.

*Chapter 2*

## THE ABSOLUTENESS OF TRUTH

"The Son of God, Jesus Christ, who was preached among you by us, even by me and Silvanus and Timothy, was not yea and nay, but in him is yea" (II Corinthians 1:19).

"If any man willeth to do his will, he shall know of the teaching, whether it is of God, or whether I speak from myself" (John 7:17).

"Jesus therefore said to those Jews that had believed him, If ye abide in my word, then are ye truly my disciples; and ye shall know the truth, and the truth shall make you free" (John 8:31-32).

In Christ, all *is* amen. If it is truth, it is bound to be absolute. Truth is absolute to the Lord. He poses the question, Who may know the truth? Those who in their hearts will to do His will. As they are absolute towards God, so the truth is also absolute in them. What a worker (servant of God) fears most is lowering God's word to make it less absolute. How often truth becomes less absolute in us because of our personal feeling, our own future, some human consideration, and relationship with the world. A worker ought to keep the habit of maintaining the absoluteness of the truth. This should become a constant character trait in his life. God's truth is absolute, but sometimes it becomes relative to us. We consider what we can do as truth, and what we dislike to keep as non-essential.

We, instead of God, evaluate the worth of truth. It becomes a matter of man controlling truth instead of truth controlling man.

The absoluteness of truth is not affected by personal conduct nor by individual feeling. Whoever twists the word of God is not serviceable to Him. We should elevate our experience to meet God's word instead of lowering His truth to suit our experience. How people try to alter God's truth instead of changing their own behavior! For example, one who is impatient, frequently losing his temper, will insist that his temper is acceptable but that trying to be patient is hypocritical and false; so why should he restrain his temper? This is lowering the standard of God's truth to fit in with his behavior.

Sometimes we dare not proclaim a certain truth because we are afraid of condemning ourselves. We are in fear of light and so we keep others in darkness. How truth becomes relative! When Aaron's two sons Nadab and Abihu died because of offering strange fire, Aaron kept his silence in order to maintain the glory of God. In addition, Moses said to Aaron and his two remaining sons Eleazar and Ithamar not to let the hairs of their heads go loose: they must set aside their personal feelings and maintain God's truth (see Lev. 10.1-7). The rebellion of the Korah party was due to their ignoring the high priesthood of Aaron, and hence, they were all burnt to death. They had brought in their "self," and did not submit to truth by maintaining its absoluteness (see Num. 16.1-50). In similar manner, Saul had ill-treated David.

There are a few conditions which should be mentioned for maintaining the absoluteness of truth: (1) Never let "self" in. We must be delivered from "self" and all the people, affairs and things related to "self"; (2) we must be delivered from all natural feelings, such as love or hate, which may interfere with the truth of God; (3) we must be delivered from concerns over the gain or loss of material things; and (4) we must reject position and glory before people. Should we be able to fulfill these conditions, it will be easier for the church to fulfill its mission. Whenever there is the playing of politics, truth loses its absoluteness. Paul had to confront Peter over such a matter (see Galatians 2:11ff.). All who yield to their own feeling may not stand nor help others. We must pay any cost to maintain the truth. Some may suggest that people will be offended. But let us hold to the truth instead of considering men.[*]

---

[*] Message given on May 26, 1949.

## HOW TO EXERCISE OUR SPIRIT

How are we to exercise our spirit? How can we touch the spirit? When the disciples asked the Lord if they should call fire down from heaven to burn up the Samaritans, their wrong spirit was exposed (see Luke 9.51-56 KJV). We have neither the time with which to spend three to five months with our brothers and sisters nor do we have a physician's instruments by which to test people's spirit. It will be nearly impossible to help others if we do not know how to listen and to touch people with our spirit.

(1) Is another's spirit right or wrong? Is his word true or false? Pay attention to the spirit behind the word, not the word itself. If the spirit in a person is moving, it will show up in his attitude and intention. If your own spirit has been trained, you will be able to sense whether the spirit and the word in the other person agree. Many speak their words well but their spirit differs. For example, the word may be "love" but the heart intent of people is "hate." You will be deceived if you do not recognize what is in the other person's spirit. Some may speak humbly, yet their spirits are full of arrogance. Some may seem to be seeking after the Lord diligently, but their spirits are nonetheless full of envy; how they hope that no one else will surpass them so that they will be the only advanced people in the church. A man's spirit represents his true condition: his spirit is the very "essence" of his life: in short, it represents him.

(2) How is the difference between an arrogant or a feeble spirit: a feeble spirit needs to be strengthened, whereas an arrogant one needs to be broken.

(3) The human spirit has its characteristic. It takes its feature from the outward man — that is to say, from the soul-life of a person. For the spirit itself is neutral. If the mind of a person is energetic, you touch a big brain. Or if his emotion is strong, the spirit conveys that vigorous feeling. For when the spirit is released, it is clothed with the person's soul. It never comes forth by itself or in isolation. When the will is tenacious, the spirit will appear stubborn and stiff-necked. A meek person is easier to be entreated (see James 3.17), whereas a subjective person is not easily corrected. Our will needs to be broken. A person's *dominant characteristic* is often his *problem.* By touching one's more pronounced characteristic, you can help him. Not knowing that characteristic, you fail to find out his problem.

(4) To be strong is quite normal. But if there is abnormal growth in strong characteristics, something is wrong. Should the mind become over-active, exceeding the normal development, it will cause abnormal psychological problems. The mind may be overly-developed to the extent of suppressing the other functions of the soul. Such people will not have an easy time before God. If your spirit is only capable of coping with common spiritual problems and is unable to deal with abnormal cases, your usefulness in helping people is quite limited. Such abnormal spirits test the very foundation of your spirit. The tenderer your spirit is, the greater will be the effect of an abnormal spirit upon you. It will seem as though his abnormal condition casts its rebellion, pressure and uncleanness upon you. However, if

your spirit is strong and pure enough, you will have the strength and the proper word to deal with it.

(5) Try to detect if there be any man-made and false thing in the other person. Is there any hidden motive behind words? If you are unable to detect these things, you have no way to help. When the spirit of deception appears, you should recognize it, though you may not identify its source.

A person may have teaching yet no light. There can be a man-made attitude, ethics and words. These words are manufactured by man. They are accomplished by his own effort. They all come from self. To deal oneself with teaching is the format of theology. God, however, will *destroy* whatever is built by man's own effort. Then, He will destroy the difficulties in human nature. For wherever there is anything man-made, there is hypocrisy in the spirit. All who attempt to improve by their own self-effort can cast a deceiving spirit upon you, whether intentional or not. When deception does come, what will be your reaction? It will be one of the following: (a) You have no reaction because your feeling is so different from it; (b) you feel annoyed; or (c) you sense being defiled. It is therefore essential to keep your spirit pure.

(6) A persons inability to release his spirit is most serious. It shows either (a) he is not saved, or (b) he never has any fellowship with God's children. He has not the life of amen; that is to say, he can neither amen others nor be amened by others.

(7) A shy spirit in a person tends to be hidden away. It is quite possible that his spirit has been wounded through being misunderstood, beaten down or evil spoken of. He may have

passed through difficulties and was unjustly blamed. He thus became shy. He needs to be comforted and encouraged. Sometimes he even has to be beaten down more so as to be healed through greater wounds.

(8) Something strange in another person may happen. His spirit has launched out, yet you cannot diagnose his sickness. Nine out of ten times this is due to unrevealed hidden sin. Sometimes it can even be the symptom of a special satanic attack.

(9) A spirit "flowing with milk and honey" in another shows maturity. It is sweet as honey and nutritious as milk. It is altogether pleasant, neither sour nor unclean. This indicates that the person has traveled far on the road of spirituality. He is full of power and his supply is both tender and delicate.

After all is said and done, how are we to touch another's spirit with our spirit? This is only made possible when our outward man is broken. This does not mean that henceforth we will use our spirit automatically. For in using our spirit, we must restrain the entire outward man. All comes to rest and tranquillity. There is no interference of our thoughts and feelings. It is like a white paper waiting to be impressed by the spirit of other people.[*]

---

[*] Message given on the evening of May 26, 1949.

# PART THREE: APPROVE THE EXCELLENT

*"… so that ye may approve the things that are excellent; that ye may be sincere and void of offence unto the day of Christ."*

Philippians 1.10

*Chapter 1*

## <u>A WISH</u>

- If people notice me and praise me above the Lord himself, may the Lord cause me to fall.

- At any time that I feel great and honored, strike me, Lord, that I may fall at Your feet.

- Lord! If in the depth of my heart I am boastful, cause me to fail completely in what I have boasted.

- I would rather see my fault and confess my untrustworthiness so as not to rely on myself than to see my good and secretly boast of myself as though I am so very dependable. O Lord! Whenever I consider myself good and dependable, let what I depend on fail. When You keep me from any error, will You also keep me from daring to uplift myself before God or people? I dare not trust in "myself."

- I would rather be judged by man as lacking in zeal than to be reckoned by the Lord as being zealous apart from His will.

- Where is the aim of labor if I consider work more important than "the Lord himself"?

- Oftentimes, believers remember too well working for people or even for the Lord, but they forget to allow the Lord to work in them. When there is no work, they are troubled. Why not give the Lord a chance to work!

- God's provision cannot be seen without ascending Mount Moriah; but how few are those who go up (see Gen. 22.1-14). Who is willing to ascend? Let us go up to the mountain of the Lord!

- It must be a matter of "doing it after you know it" and not simply a matter of "saying it when you know it."

- To hate oneself after being put to shame cannot be reckoned as being for the glory of the Lord. In reality, this is nothing but loving one's self rather than hating oneself.

- People sigh and mourn with tears when what the Lord has ordained to be destroyed is destroyed. Should I do the same if I am considerate of the Lord's heart?

- To lay the sacrifice on the altar which sanctifies it is easier than to tie the sacrifice to the altar and leave it there (see again Gen. 22.9f.).

*Chapter 2*

## AN ALL-ROUND VIEW OF THE CROSS

- The greatest act of denial in the universe is the cross, for by it God gets rid of all things which do not belong to Him.

- The cross is the power of God, translating us from Adam to Christ.

- Whom God needs are people who have passed through the cross and are being dealt with by it.

- The blood obtains forgiveness for us; the cross delivers us from what we formerly were.

- The blood deals with what we did; the cross deals with what we were. As the blood takes away our sins, so the cross strikes at the source of sinning.

- The cross will not shake up things which come from God; rather, the cross finishes all things which come from men.

- It is useless to confess and speak out with the mouth if one rejects in his heart the principle of the judgment of self by the cross.

- Whatever arises from God will not be slain by the cross, whereas anything which can be slain by the cross must come from man.

- Without willingly and gladly accepting the principle of the cross, you cannot see the effect of the cross in your life; for its principle rests in denying self and trusting God.

- In us there is much refuse — many things not of God, many things not glorifying Him; so God uses the cross to purify us that we might be pure gold.

- Whatever comes out of man is finished after passing through the cross; whatever is of God cannot be touched by death.

- The cross is not for giving out things; it instead takes things away.

- Were we to be dealt with by the cross we would lose our self-confidence and dare not boast again. If we are proud of our ability, we know nothing of the cross.

- By the cross believers are delivered from the sins of the flesh; it is also through the cross that they are freed from the righteousness of the flesh. If believers walk after the Holy Spirit, they will not follow the flesh and sin nor will they walk after the righteousness of the flesh.

- The Holy Spirit can work only through the cross. Apart from the cross, the Holy Spirit has no other instrument by which to work.

- Even though what was accomplished on the cross is in fact complete, what one actually experiences is nevertheless according to his knowledge and faith in the cross.

- We should daily live out the cross in our lives.

- Each time we bypass the cross, each time we nourish our soul life and preserve it.

- The cross does not count how many things have been dealt with, since it deals with the entire "old creation."

- We should allow the power of the cross to cut us like the knife in circumcision that cuts away the flesh.

- The cross has its special mission and its special work in us. May we not let the cross pass us by.

- To lie on the altar is what we ought to do; using the knife to separate our spirit and soul is what our High Priest will do.

- The effect of the cross will not be manifested in the lives of those who trust in their own works.

- None who is opinionated and believes in his own strength knows the cross. The cross has never done any work in such a life.

- Each time a believer keeps his mouth shut in tribulation can see the cross working in him.

- The people of God have a mark, a certain characteristic, which is, a denying the flesh, they not trusting in the power of the flesh. For God's people are those who have cut off any confidence in the flesh.

- To cut away the confidence in the flesh is to cut off a person's natural strength so that he dare not speak or act carelessly before God. Instead, he trembles before Him.

- In delivering us from the power of sin, God uses the cross to crucify us, not to strengthen our old man. Instead of helping us to do things, the cross forbids us to do anything out from our self-life.

- Not until we thoroughly know the cross will we be able to come into that blessed place of trusting God.

- All which happens in our lives are the fruits of the working of the cross of Christ; we must not neglect any of them.

- Historically, Pentecost comes after Calvary; even so, in spiritual experience, the filling of the Holy Spirit also comes after the bearing of the cross.

- Whenever the cross has done its work, then will we be ready to receive the power of the Holy Spirit.

- Do not admire success and greatness; pay attention only to see whether our old creation — all which comes with natural birth — has passed through the cross.

- Wherever the scar of the cross is missing, the anointing of the Holy Spirit is lacking.

- All works done without the cross and the Holy Spirit are dead works.

- Always remember! If no thorn, then no grace nor power. Your field of service will also be very narrow.

- Each and every trial causes you to fall down by the piercing of the thorn, thus enabling you to experience the grace of the thorn.

- May we let God break in today so that we dare not have any independent action and attitude.

- If I do not have the death of the cross, others will not obtain the life of the cross.

- If we ourselves are not crucified, how can we give life to others by proclaiming the cross?

- The cross is a fact. If you proclaim it with knowledge only, you can only spread the theory of the cross. You are not able to pass on the power and life of the cross.

- The cross we proclaim demands that we first be crucified.

- The cross must work so deeply that you are willing to accept gladly the part God has apportioned to you, and let Him take care of His glory.

## THE BODY OF CHRIST

A certain spiritual missionary told me one of her experiences. She said the following: She formerly was in a certain denomination and was assigned to teach in a certain Christian school. Because of her love for the Lord, she especially worked among the students to save the lost and edify the believers. And the Lord had greatly blessed the labor. Largely for this reason, she incurred the jealousy of her colleagues.

Later on, one accused her of many sins before the annual meeting of her denomination. The committee members, without announcing the name of the accuser nor disclosing the reason for her being accused, sent people to notify her that the denomination had expelled her and asked her to get ready to return to England. She was expelled! When she heard it, it was like a thunder out of the blue, not knowing where it came from. She therefore requested the committee, saying that she was willing to go back to her country, but they should tell her who was her accuser and what were the sins she committed for which she was expelled and ordered home. No criminal would ever be sent to the gallows without knowing his crime. However, they refused to tell. Later on, she committed this matter to God in prayer. Under such great pressure, she wept before the Lord. She knew she was expelled without cause. She thought about herself: what would happen to her name hereafter, how people would disdain her; the committee must reveal the real fact so as to clear the case. The more she thought of her future, the more her pride within her would not let the case rest.

Yet in prayer, she seemed to see the Lord! And the Lord taught her, saying: "You belong to Me and the one who accuses you also belongs to Me. I am the Head, you both are my members. Look at My hand; what difference is there to Me the Head, if the thumb is hurt or the middle finger is hurt? They both cause Me, the Head, pain. Whether you are hurt or she is hurt, all cause pain. So, why must you strive to clarify? Why must you complain? My child, be silent! Put your future into My hand!" So, she returned to England. She incurred the misunderstandings and the despising from many people, they assuming that she had committed some unspeakable sins in China! Later, however, she came back to China and served the Lord in Fukien Province for about twenty years. None of her former colleagues remain in China anymore.

## Chapter 4

## AN UNDELIVERED SERMON

A certain professor of a certain university was quite famous and was greatly admired. One day he was sitting in his study. On his desk there were many, many books, except that one book – the Bible – was missing. Actually he was preparing for a sermon to be delivered on the coming Lord's day, for he had been invited to speak in the university chapel. He was aware that many would be there to hear him. The chancellor, the other professors, and hundreds of students would all attend the service. Even famous specialists and merchants of the city would also attend to hear him. This magnificent chapel was famous for its excellent music in the morning service; because of which, society people often were also present. For all these reasons, this professor felt he must try his best in preparing his sermon. He knew he was well known. Some of his colleagues had spoken there before and had been severely criticized. He must not commit the same mistake. He needed to say something novel yet current. Clearly he was looking for people's praise, not God's approval.

He sat there covering his head with his hands, quietly talking to himself at times. Then he uttered, "I have it." He took a sheet of paper and wrote some letters on it: "New Teaching." He said to himself, "This is to be the topic of my speech – New Teaching." Two weeks previously, a preacher had preached there. People criticized him for inclining to the old school of thought. Some of what he had said was ridiculed by people. The younger people labeled him as "old fashioned". But now this professor was preparing to speak on the New Idea: He would have the opportunity to refute what the previous preacher had said. He knew for sure that this would be what the audience would love to hear.

So now he began to write down what he intended to speak. He needed, of course, to have a scripture verse, for according to the university's chapel custom, there should be at least one scripture verse to serve as the basis for the Lord's day morning service. What scripture verse should he pick? Finally he chose Acts 17.19 which reads: "they took hold of him [Paul], and brought him unto the Areopagus, saying, May we know what this new teaching is, which is spoken by thee?" The professor said to himself: "It is fortunate I have selected this verse, for I have now the opportunity to show off my knowledge of some Greek history and literature." He quickly wrote it down.

After he wrote down something about the Areopagus hill and various Greek philosophies, he began to put down as the first section of his sermon – the "Old Concept." Then he wrote: "In this matter of religion, there were old concepts. But in the light of modern scientific research these old concepts can no longer be accepted in our new age. What our ancestors believed is today too old fashioned; they are unfit for the new generation. Were former great theologians to be able to be here today, they too would reject their old faith and agree to our new teaching."

Now what were these "old concepts"? Here he had the chance to refute what the previous preacher had said before. He thought of finding in this so-called infallible book — the Bible — some scornful beliefs. He assumed that "in this world there is no such mistake-proof thing for mistake-proof means something perfect, which is impossible. The world cannot have a book without any mistake, neither would it contain any infallible truth, nor have in it a person void of

error. Even Christ is not without mistake; he too had faults."
He further insisted: "Jesus was supposedly born of a virgin.
This kind of belief cannot be explained by science. There is
no proof of it in world history; therefore, it is merely a
legend. And as to the concept of resurrection, this too is
opposed by great scholars, and science knows nothing of it.
Intelligent people have no doubt that the so-called
resurrection of Jesus does not really refer to his being raised
from the dead; rather, it refers to his conduct, his personality,
his teaching and his example. The old thought suggests that
after death there is heaven and a 'place of punishment' [he
used this phrase as a substitute for hell]. Such an old belief is
also beyond reason. We do not know what the future holds.
There might be a next life after death, but it can never be
like the after-life spoken of in the Bible because we cannot
be sure of that."

All these words constituted the first section of his
written sermon. He was now going to write the second
section, which was to be entitled, "The New Teaching." So
he wrote: "We are like the Athenians of old still seeking for
new things. We are still in this process of searching." As he
set down on paper this new evolutionary theology, he wrote
still more.

Just as he wrote further, however, suddenly two little
hands embraced his neck. This was his eleven-year-old only-
begotten daughter. She had entered his study, but her father
had not paid any attention to it. She said to him, "Daddy,
lunch is ready. Mother has called you three times; we
thought you were asleep."

He pointed to his draft and said, "No, I had not fallen
asleep. I have been extremely busy. Do you know that your
dad is going to preach in that big chapel next Sunday
morning?"

At the meal, he talked of nothing but his sermon: how he had found this subject and that he had to spend that whole afternoon and evening to finish its draft. At that moment, however, his daughter said to him: "But, Papa! You have already promised me that this afternoon you would take me to that hilltop. Now how about it? Please, Papa, take me there!" He shook his head, saying, "I am afraid you shall have to wait till next week, that is, after I have preached my sermon. It is truly regretful. But today is already Wednesday. Besides my teaching assignments, I will have to spend all my extra time preparing the sermon." His daughter was truly disappointed and, almost broke out crying. At that moment her mother tried to comfort her, saying to her, "Daddy will for sure bring you to that hilltop to see the cemetery and the old farm house."

That afternoon the professor busily wrote his sermon till midnight. He changed his draft several times. Then he finally said, "Now I am able to finish the draft. Tomorrow, day after tomorrow and Saturday, I will study it and thoroughly memorize it." After saying this, he left the study and went to his adjoining bedroom to sleep.

Next morning, his wife came to him earlier than usual and informed him that his daughter had not slept well last night and ran a fever. It was probably something wrong with her gall, but she had already been given the medicine she usually took for this problem. Immediately he went to see his child, and the child said, "Papa, had you taken me to that hilltop to see the cemetery and the farm house, I would not be sick this morning." He kissed her and said, "Next week, I will take you there."

He returned to his study and busily engaged himself once again in the New Teaching sermon to be preached. He had a class at two o'clock in the afternoon but now he focused on his sermon. Near noontime, his wife knocked on his study door and entered, saying: "I really do not want to disturb you, but Carol [the child's name] seems to be seriously ill. Her fever now runs to one hundred and three. She constantly mentions going to the hilltop. She is now unconscious." Immediately he telephoned the doctor, asking him to come at once. After lunch, the doctor arrived. After examination, he said that her illness was very serious, her temperature was very high, and that her throat was swollen. At dusk, the doctor came again. The child had become worse. He diagnosed it as throat fever. In the evening, he gave her an injection of vaccine against the fever. But the little girl's physical stamina was now low; and the high fever did not subside the whole night through. Her parents watched over her with great anxiety. The father (the professor) frequently ran to his study, knelt before his desk upon which was his sermon draft. He secretly shed tears, crying aloud, "O God, if You really hear prayers, please save my child, my only child, Carol!"

Early the next morning, the doctor again came to see her. He was disappointed as he examined her. The child was not better. So, he invited several other doctors in for consultation. The child was breathing heavily and often muttered, "Papa, go to the hill." The faces of the doctors grew very serious; they decided to stay there for some hours.

This professor again returned to his study. He wanted to pray, but he could not pray. After an hour, an elderly doctor who was a Christian knocked on the door of the study. The professor quickly got up and asked, "Doctor! How is she? Have you healed her? Will she be well?" The elderly man looked at him without saying anything and soon bowed his head. Finally, he said, "Professor, come and see her smiling face. How sweet it is. A Christian thinks this is beautiful."

Before he had ended speaking, the professor rushed to the room of his sick daughter. The child lay there with her eyes closed but her face showed her smiling. But she was now dead.

This sad news spread quickly. Among the students of the professors there were a few truly zealous in the Lord. In the evening they gathered by the windows of the professor's study and sang softly:

Abide with me: fast falls the eventide;
The darkness deepens; Lord, with me abide!
When other helpers fail, and comforts flee,
Help of the helpless, oh, abide with me.

Swift to its close ebbs out life's little day;
Earth's joys grow dim, its glories pass away;
Change and decay in all around I see;
O thou who changest not, abide with me.

They did not know that the professor was sitting by the side of the desk in the study. His sermon draft was cast aside, and all the reference books had been returned to his book shelves. All he now held in his hand was a Bible. Unconsciously he turned to one passage to read (at that moment his eyes were full of tears): "Let not your heart be troubled: believe in God, believe also in me. In my Father's house are many mansions; if it were not so, I would have told you; for I go to prepare a place for you. And if I go and prepare a place for you, I come again, and will receive you unto myself; that where I am, there ye may be also" (John 14.1-3).

During that same moment he heard the hymn-singing outside (at that moment he was quietly crying):

Hold thou thy cross before my closing eyes;
Shine through the gloom, and point me to the skies;
Heaven's morning breaks, and earth's vain shadows flee;
In life, in death, O Lord, abide with me.

He opened up his Bible and again read: "I am the resurrection, and the life: he that believeth on me, though he die, yet shall he live; and whosoever liveth and believeth on me shall never die. Believest thou this?" (John 11.25-26). With trembling voice he cried out, saying: "O Lord, I believe." His eyes were immediately opened. He saw the vanity of this new teaching; deep within his heart he sensed that such new teaching gave him neither hope nor comfort. What he formerly believed in gave no life, no hope, no supply of comfort at his time of sorrow. He knelt down in prayer. Ah, what a prayer! He confessed his fault and cast himself into the embrace of His Lord who had forgiven him.

Monday morning they went to the hilltop. The coffin in which the child was laid was covered with white flowers. Four professors carried the coffin. The preacher read from the Bible: "this we say unto you by the word of the Lord, that we that are alive, that are left unto the coming of the Lord, shall in no wise precede them that are fallen asleep. For the Lord himself shall descend from heaven, with a shout, with the voice of the archangel, and with the trump of God: and the dead in Christ shall rise first; then we that are alive, that are left, shall together with them be caught up in the clouds, to meet the Lord in the air: and so shall we ever be with the Lord. Wherefore comfort one another with these words" (1 Thess. 4.15-18).

After the coffin was lowered into the grave, the father came forward with his head lowered and stood before the crowd, saying, "Friends, my beloved child is gone. She is now with the Lord who has died for her. I want to confess this Lord as my Savior before this open grave. The Lord left the glory of heaven and came down to earth to die for our sins. He was buried, and on the third day he was resurrected: He is coming to receive us to His glorious self. At that time, my child will again be embraced in my bosom. This faith is what I constantly rejected before my students and colleagues, but now He is the only belief that gives me peace and hope."[*]

---

[*] This story was told by Watchman Nee in China, and is now translated into English. He might have read it in English somewhere, but the original cannot be found. — *Translator*

# TITLES AVAILABLE
## from Christian Fellowship Publishers

### By Watchman Nee

ORDER FROM:  11515 Allecingie Parkway Richmond, VA 23235
www.c-f-p.com – 804-794-5333

# TITLES AVAILABLE
# from Christian Fellowship Publishers

## By Stephen Kaung

"But We See Jesus"
—*the Life of the Lord Jesus*
Discipled to Christ
—*As Seen in the Life of Simon Peter*
God's Purpose for the Family
The Gymnasium of Christ
In the Footsteps of Christ
The Key to "Revelation" – Vol. 1
The Key to "Revelation" – Vol. 2
Men After God's Own Heart
—*Eight Biographies from the Book of Genesis*
New Covenant Living & Ministry
Now We See the Church
—*the Life of the Church, the Body of Christ*
Shepherding
The Songs of Degrees
—*Meditations on Fifteen Psalms*
The Splendor of His Ways
—*Seeing the Lord's End in Job*

The "God Has Spoken" Series
Seeing Christ in the Old Testament, Part One
Seeing Christ in the Old Testament, Part Two
Seeing Christ in the New Testament

ORDER FROM:  11515 Allecingie Parkway Richmond, VA 23235
www.c-f-p.com – 804-794-5333